Dealing with Feeling...

Proud

Isabel Thomas

Illustrated by Clare Elsom

Heinemann
LIBRARY
Chicago, Illinois

T0052146

© 2013 Heinemann Library
an imprint of Capstone Global Library, LLC
Chicago, Illinois

All rights reserved. No part of this publication may be reproduced or transmitted in any form or by any means, electronic or mechanical, including photocopying, recording, taping, or any information storage and retrieval system, without permission in writing from the publisher.

Edited by Dan Nunn, Rebecca Rissman, and Catherine Veitch
Designed by Philippa Jenkins
Original illustrations © Clare Elsom
Illustrated by Clare Elsom
Production by Victoria Fitzgerald
Originated by Capstone Global Library, Ltd.

Library of Congress Cataloging-in-Publication Data
Thomas, Isabel, 1980-
Proud / Isabel Thomas.
p. cm.—(Dealing with feeling)
Includes bibliographical references and index.
ISBN 978-1-4329-7107-6 (hb)—ISBN 978-1-4329-7116-8 (pb) 1. Self-esteem in children—Juvenile literature. 2. Self-esteem—Juvenile literature. 3. Pride and vanity—Juvenile literature. I. Title.
BF723.S3T56 2013
152.4—dc23 2012008394

Every effort has been made to contact copyright holders of material reproduced in this book. Any omissions will be rectified in subsequent printings if notice is given to the publisher.

All the Internet addresses (URLs) given in this book were valid at the time of going to press. However, due to the dynamic nature of the Internet, some addresses may have changed, or sites may have changed or ceased to exist since publication. While the author and publisher regret any inconvenience this may cause readers, no responsibility for any such changes can be accepted by either the author or the publisher.

Printed in the United States 5920

Contents

What Is Pride? 4
What Makes People Feel Proud? 6
What Does Pride Feel Like? 8
How Can Pride Make Other People Feel? 10
What If Other People Do Not Seem Pleased for Me? 12
How Should I Deal with Pride? 14
What If I Have Nothing to Feel Proud About? ... 16
What Can I Do to Feel Proud? 18
How Can I Help Other People to Feel Proud? .. 20
Make a Pride Toolbox 22
Glossary 23
Find Out More 24
Index 24

Some words are shown in bold, **like this**. Find out what they mean in the glossary on page 23.

What Is Pride?

Pride is a **feeling**. It is normal to have many kinds of feelings every day.

Some feelings are nice to have. Pride is a nice feeling. We feel proud when we are pleased with ourselves.

What Makes People Feel Proud?

When somebody says that we are kind or look good, we feel proud. It is nice to get a **compliment**.

We feel proud when we do something well or achieve a goal. We feel proud when we are brave and do something that scares us.

What Does Pride Feel Like?

When you are proud, you feel good about yourself.

You might feel more **confident**. Pride can make you want to work hard and do well again.

How Can Pride Make Other People Feel?

People show their **feelings** in different ways. Feeling proud can make us act like we are more important than other people.

It might look as if we are **showing off**. This can make other people feel jealous, angry, or sad.

What If Other People Do Not Seem Pleased for Me?

It is normal to feel proud when you do something well. It can be hard when other people do not seem pleased for you.

Remember that they have **feelings**, too. They might feel sad that they are not the best this time.

How Should I Deal with Pride?

Sometimes we feel proud because we have something that other people **admire.** It is nice to feel proud. It is not nice to **boast** about what you have.

When you feel proud, remember not to **show off.** You can be a good friend by sharing what you have.

What If I Have Nothing to Feel Proud About?

Everyone has something to feel proud about. Ask your friends why they like hanging out with you.

Ask your family what they like most about you. You can be proud of being a great brother or sister, a great son or daughter, or a great friend.

What Can I Do to Feel Proud?

You can feel proud by working hard in school. You can feel proud when you help out at home.

You do not have to BE *the* best to be proud of yourself. You just have to DO your best.

How Can I Help Other People to Feel Proud?

You can make people feel proud by giving them **compliments**. It is nice to make other people feel good about themselves.

If you are good at doing something, try teaching other people how to do it. Everyone feels proud when they learn something new.

Make a Pride Toolbox

Write down some tips to help you feel proud every day.

Glossary

admire think that something is good

boast talk about things that you have or can do in a way that makes other people feel bad

compliment when you tell somebody something that you like about him or her

confident feeling that you can do something well

feeling something that happens inside our minds. It can affect our bodies and the way we behave.

show off boast about things that you have or can do

Find Out More

Books

Ludwig, Trudy. *Better Than You.* Berkeley: Tricycle, 2011.

Medina, Sarah. *Proud (Feelings).* Chicago: Heinemann Library, 2007.

Internet sites

Facthound offers a safe, fun way to find Internet sites related to this book. All of the sites on Facthound have been researched by our staff.

Here's all you do:
Visit www.facthound.com
Type in this code: 9781432971076

Index

being kind 6
doing well 7, 12
feeling good 8, 20
feeling pleased 5
great friend 17
not the best 13, 19
sharing 15
showing off 11, 15
working hard 9, 18